David Farragut

A Proud Heritage The Hispanic Library

David Farragut

First Admiral of the U.S. Navy

R. Conrad Stein

Content Adviser: Fred L. Schultz
Editor in Chief, *Naval History*
Buda, Texas

Published in the United States of America by The Child's World®
PO Box 326 • Chanhassen, MN 55317-0326 • 800-599-READ • www.childsworld.com

Acknowledgments
   The Child's World®: Mary Berendes, Publishing Director

   Editorial Directions, Inc.: E. Russell Primm, Editorial Director; Pam Rosenberg, Project
   Editor; Katie Marsico, Associate Editor; Matt Messbarger, Editorial Assistant; Susan Hindman,
   Copyeditor; Lucia Raatma, Proofreader; Stephen Carl Vender, Fact Checker; Timothy Griffin/
   IndexServ, Indexer; Dawn Friedman, Photo Researcher; Linda S. Koutris, Photo Selector

   Creative Spark: Mary Francis and Rob Court, Design and Page Production

   Cartography by XNR Productions, Inc.

Photos
   Cover: portrait of David Farragut circa 1840, Bettmann/Corbis

   Réunion des Musées Nationaux/Art Resource, NY: 17; National Portrait Gallery, Smithsonian
   Institution/Art Resource, NY: 36; Corbis: 10, 26, 28, 32; Abbie Enock, Travel Ink/Corbis: 18;
   Museum of the City of New York/Corbis: 27; Hulton|Archive/Getty Images: 9, 30; the Granger
   Collection, New York: 13, 20, 24, 29, 31; Department of the Navy, Naval Historical Center: 12,
   15, 19, 35; North Wind Picture Archives: 8, 14, 21, 34; Stock Montage, Inc.: 7, 22.

Library of Congress Cataloging-in-Publication Data
   Stein, R. Conrad.
      David Farragut : first admiral of the U.S. Navy / by R. Conrad Stein.
         p. cm. — (A proud heritage)
      Includes bibliographical references and index.
      ISBN 1-59296-383-8 (Library Bound : alk. paper) 1. Farragut, David Glasgow, 1801–1870—
   Juvenile literature. 2. United States—History—Civil War, 1861–1865—Naval operations—
   Juvenile literature. 3. United States—History, Naval—To 1900—Juvenile literature. 4.
   Admirals—United States—Biography—Juvenile literature. 5. United States. Navy—
   Biography—Juvenile literature. I. Title. II. Proud heritage (Child's World (Firm))
      E467.1.F23S76 2005
      973.7'58'092—dc22   2004018045

Chapter One

"Damn the Torpedoes . . ."

"So daring an attempt was never made in any country but ours, and was never successfully made by any commander except Farragut who . . . proved himself one of the greatest naval commanders the world has ever seen."

> (Lieutenant John Kinney, who served under Rear Admiral David Glasgow Farragut in the Battle of Mobile Bay, August 1864.)

By the summer of 1864, the American Civil War (1861–1865) had been raging for more than three years. Thousands of Americans had died in the conflict. The war at sea was brutal, too, as the navy of the North tried to blockade and capture the South's port cities. Sea battles along the southern coast saw gun duels between warships and the powerful forts standing onshore. Armored vessels called ironclads had

Many fierce battles were fought at sea as the Union navy tried to capture Confederate port cities.

recently been introduced and added to the danger of naval combat. The waters in many southern ports were laced with mines, which in those days were called torpedoes. When a ship struck an explosive torpedo, it could sink in minutes, carrying most of its crew to the harbor floor.

On August 5, 1864, another bloody sea battle **loomed** at Mobile Bay, Alabama. The Northern side— the Union—had assembled a fleet of 14 wooden ships

Torpedoes, or mines, were used during the Civil War to keep enemy ships from entering harbors.

and four ironclad vessels. Blocking passage to Mobile Bay was the South's Fort Morgan—a Confederate stronghold—which could aim 47 guns at any fleet. Within the bay were several Confederate ships, including the *Tennessee,* perhaps the most powerful ironclad on Earth.

Commanding the Union fleet was David Glasgow Farragut. At age 63, he was one of the oldest military leaders on either side. Farragut had been a seaman for more than 50 years. Despite the guns of Fort Morgan to the east and Fort Gaines to the west and the Confederate ships, he was determined to carry out his mission. At dawn, Farragut ordered his fleet to sail into Mobile Bay.

Ironclad ships led Farragut's attacking **flotilla.** Gunfire erupted like thunder on the summer morning.

Union sailors crowd the deck of a ship during the Civil War.

The Battle of Mobile Bay was fierce and many lives were lost.

Fort Morgan's cannons poured shell after shell at the invading vessels. Most of the shells bounced off the ironclads' thick armor. But the ironclads were far slower than wooden ships. This was a distinct disadvantage in battle. Soon the wooden warships overtook the ironclads and dodged fire from the Confederate fort.

War at sea in those days was so ghastly it is nearly impossible to picture its horror today. Shells tore through the Union's wooden ships, mangling sailors crowded in the compartments below. One officer said the scene was "sickening beyond the power of words to portray. Shot after shot came through the side, mowing down the men, deluging the decks with blood . . . so thickly that it was difficult to stand on deck, so slippery it was."

The Battle of Mobile Bay appeared to be a disastrous defeat for the Union fleet and its commander, David Farragut. Murderous fire poured onto the vessels from

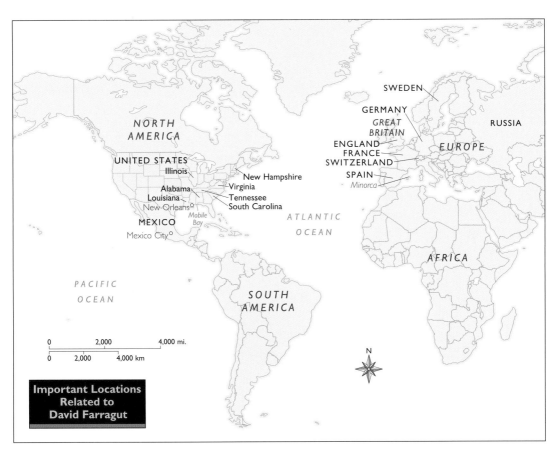

David Farragut spent almost his entire life serving in the U.S. Navy. He distinguished himself in battle during the Civil War, especially in the Battle of Mobile Bay.

Fort Morgan. Dozens of sailors were killed or wounded on the bloody decks. Worst of all, the fleet was approaching the floating mines, the dreaded torpedoes. The leading Union ironclad, the *Tecumseh,* struck a torpedo and an explosion rang out. The *Tecumseh* sank before most of its crew could abandon ship. An officer on a trailing vessel said, "[The *Tecumseh*'s] stern lifted high in the air with the propeller still revolving, and the ship pitched out of sight like an arrow

Most of the Tecumseh*'s crew was killed when the ship sank during the Battle of Mobile Bay.*

twanged from the bow."
Ninety sailors of the
Tecumseh's 114-man crew
were killed.

With shells bursting
around him, Admiral
Farragut climbed the
mainmast of his ship to
get a better view of the
battle. A young sailor
scrambled up behind
Farragut and tied him to
the mast with a line. The
sailor was afraid the older
man would become dizzy

Farragut climbed the rigging of his ship to get a better view of the battle at Mobile Bay.

from the height and fall. Ahead, the Union vessels
inched along because their captains feared striking
more torpedoes. The barrel-shaped mines floated near
the surface and were almost impossible to see from the
deck of a ship.

The fear of torpedoes was turning this battle into a
disaster for Farragut's fleet. As the ships crawled over
the surface, they made perfect targets for Fort Morgan's
guns. Perched high on his mast, Admiral Farragut bowed
his head and said a prayer. Then he is said to have

The USS Hartford *collides with the CSS* Tennessee *during the Battle of Mobile Bay.*

cupped his hands to his mouth and yelled out an order that has echoed forever in American history: "Damn the torpedoes. Full speed ahead!"

Farragut's ship took the lead and sped into the bay. Below decks, terrified sailors heard torpedoes rubbing against the sides of their ship. Fortunately, the torpedoes failed to explode. Other ships in the Union fleet followed their commander. Guns on the Union vessels pounded Fort Morgan as they passed.

Once out of range of the fort, the Union flotilla faced a new enemy. A powerful Confederate ironclad **ram,** the *Tennessee,* now confronted them. Union ships surrounded the armored giant, peppering her with gunfire. The shells thumped harmlessly off the Confederate vessel's iron sides. Finally, a lucky shot severed the *Tennessee*'s rudder chain, rendering her unable to steer. The *Tennessee*'s captain raised the white flag, surrendering his ship to Farragut. With the battle concluded, Farragut wrote a letter to his wife. He said humbly, "The Almighty has smiled at me once more."

The Confederate ironclad ram, the Tennessee, *was captured during the Battle of Mobile Bay.*

Chapter Two

Heritage of Spain and the Sea

Who was this American hero who damned the torpedoes and led his men to victory in Mobile Bay? His lifetime of service to the United States Navy was not surprising—the sea was part of the Farragut family heritage.

David Farragut's father, Jorge Farragut, was a Spaniard who came from Minorca, an island in the Mediterranean Sea. In 1775, Jorge Farragut was the captain of a small merchant ship in New Orleans. There he heard the shocking news that the American colonies had broken away from England and declared their independence. This action triggered the American Revolutionary War (1775–1783).

The elder Farragut won the favor of the Americans when he sailed his ship into Charleston, South Carolina, bringing a supply of precious cannons. At the end of

Jorge Farragut, David Farragut's father, was the captain of a merchant ship that sailed from the port of New Orleans (above).

The island of Minorca is one of the Balearics, a group of islands that lie east of Spain in the Mediterranean Sea. In the early 1200s, Spain gained control of the islands. But the Balearics were an important naval base for fleets operating in the Mediterranean. Great Britain controlled the islands for much of the 1700s. Today, the Balearics are among Europe's prime tourist attractions. The island group is known for its gentle climate and marvelous beaches. Many of the islanders work in tourist restaurants and hotels.

the war, he was given a large grant of land in what later became the state of Tennessee. By that time, Jorge had Americanized his name to George Farragut.

After settling in the United States, George Farragut married Elizabeth Shine. On July 5, 1801, their second son, James Glasgow Farragut, was born. Navy commander

David Porter was a close friend of the Farragut family. When James was only seven years old, his mother died, and the Porter family adopted him. To honor his new family, James changed his name to David Glasgow Farragut.

There was no question that David Farragut would seek a career at sea. With the help of the Porter family, he was appointed a midshipman in the U.S. Navy. A midshipman is an officer in training. The midshipman must give orders to the crew and expects those orders to be carried out. Ten-year-old Midshipman David Farragut was small for his age, weighing about 70 pounds (32 kilograms). How could he be the boss over **burly** sailors who were older and far stronger than he was? The details of his leadership qualities

David Porter was born in 1780 in Boston, Massachusetts.

are unknown, but it is safe to say that even as a boy, David Glasgow Farragut learned how to command.

His first service was on an American warship called the *Essex*. When Farragut was 11, the *Essex* battled British ships during the War of 1812 (1812–1815). If the boy sailor dreamed of finding glory in war, those dreams were shattered on his first day of

Young Men at Sea

Today, it seems shocking that David Farragut became a navy man at the age of 10. But in those days, it was not uncommon for a boy to go to sea at such an early age. All naval ships had chaplains who served as teachers as well as preachers. One of the chaplains' jobs was to teach reading and writing to young members of the crew.

David Farragut's first naval service was on the Essex, *pictured here during its battle with the* Phoebe *in March 1814 during the War of 1812.*

naval combat. In March 1814, the *Essex* was locked in a gun duel with a heavily armed British ship called the *Phoebe.* British cannon shells swept the decks of the *Essex* and slammed into her sides. Years later, Farragut wrote, "I shall never forget the horrid impression made upon me at the sight of the first man I had ever seen killed. He was a boat-swain's mate, and was fearfully mangled. It staggered and sickened me. . . ."

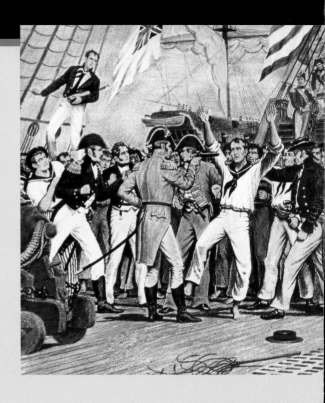

In the early 1800s, the British navy claimed the right to stop foreign ships operating on the high seas and impress their seamen. Impressing sailors meant forcing them to serve on British ships. Often, the British navy impressed men on American ships. American outrage over this practice was a major cause of the War of 1812, fought between Great Britain and the United States. Lasting from 1812 to 1815, it was largely a naval war, with battles fought on the oceans and in the Great Lakes.

After the War of 1812, Farragut remained in the U.S. Navy. Peacetime naval service was routine, and promotions were slow. By the time he was 24, after almost 14 years of service, Farragut was still a midshipman. Still, the sea was an **environment** he loved. He served in the Mediterranean and touched upon the Balearic Islands, the birthplace of his father. In his spare time, he studied foreign languages. He became fluent in several languages, including Spanish. Finally, the promotions came. Farragut made lieutenant in 1825. He was named commander in 1841 and was promoted to captain in 1855.

As Farragut climbed through the ranks, his country slipped steadily into civil war. For years, the burning question of slavery divided the nation into two hostile camps: the North (which generally opposed slavery) and the South (which hoped to preserve slavery and states' rights). In 1858, Abraham Lincoln, a young politician from Illinois, warned, "A house divided against itself cannot stand. I believe this government cannot endure permanently half slave and half free."

Husband and Father

David Farragut was married twice. After his first wife died at a young age, he married Virginia Dorcas Loyall, a well-bred lady from an old southern family. The couple had a son, Loyall Farragut, who wrote a biography detailing his father's exploits at sea.

In 1860, Lincoln was elected president of the United States, and less than six months later, the nation exploded into war.

Abraham Lincoln was born in Kentucky in 1809. Elected president in 1860, he was shot by John Wilkes Booth on April 14, 1865, and died the next day.

Chapter Three

The Civil War at Sea

David Farragut lived for many years in Virginia. Despite his southern background, he chose to join the Union navy. He showed his loyalty to the Union by giving up his house in Norfolk, Virginia, when the war began. Farragut was 60 years old, but he was in outstanding physical condition. He celebrated each birthday by doing handstands.

At the beginning of the war, President Abraham Lincoln announced a **blockade** of the entire southern coast, from Virginia down to Texas. This meant Union ships were to patrol the waters outside of Confederate port cities to prevent vessels from bringing in supplies. Such a blockade was a gigantic effort. The southern coastline stretched 3,500 miles (5,630 kilometers) and included more than 100 port cities and harbors.

Farragut's troops on shore after the capture of New Orleans.

Farragut was awarded a difficult assignment. He was to capture the port city of New Orleans, Louisiana, and then sail up the Mississippi River to conquer the Confederate forts at Vicksburg, Mississippi. For the operation, he was given a fleet of wooden ships, some of which were steam powered. His was the largest war fleet ever assembled in the Americas.

To capture New Orleans, Farragut had to move his fleet past two powerful Confederate forts that stood on opposite sides of the Mississippi. The forts **bristled** with guns. Commander Farragut ordered his sailors to

The Civil War coincided with two developments in naval warships: steam power and armor. For hundreds of years, sailors around the world fought on wooden warships driven by sails. The United States did not invent steam-powered, ironclad ships. But the first battle between such armored giants was fought during the American Civil War.

On March 8, 1862, a Confederate ironclad called the *Virginia* (formerly the Union steam frigate *Merrimack)* steamed into Hampton Roads, Virginia, and easily sank two wooden warships belonging to the Union navy. The next day, the *Virginia* returned, only to find a Union ironclad, the *Monitor,* waiting to meet it. A gun battle broke out, and the two ships pounded each other for the next four hours. Although both vessels scored direct hits, no damage was done as one cannon shell after another simply bounced off its foe's iron plating. The battle ended with both ships withdrawing and neither side able to claim victory. But in one day, wooden warships became **obsolete.** After the clash between the *Monitor* and the *Virginia,* navies throughout the world scrapped wooden warships and began to build ironclads.

David Farragut stands on the deck of the Hartford *with Captain Percival Drayton.*

wrap heavy chains around the sides of their wooden ships to offer some protection from enemy cannon shells. On the dark night of April 24, 1862, his fleet approached the forts. The night was suddenly lit with gunfire as Confederate cannons bombarded Farragut's fleet. One observer wrote, "Imagine all the earthquakes in the world, and all the thunder and lightnings together in the space of two miles [3.2 km], all going off at once."

In the heat of this battle, a small Confederate boat pushed a flaming raft into the side of Farragut's command ship, the *Hartford*. Flames licked up the *Hartford*'s wooden sides and threatened to engulf the ship. Farragut shouted to a gun crew, "Don't flinch from that fire, boys. There's a hotter fire than that for those who don't do their duty." Heroically, the *Hartford* crew doused the fire. Farragut then led his fleet past the forts and up the Mississippi toward New Orleans. To his surprise, the city itself was undefended, and Farragut forced it to surrender.

This was a grand prize, because New Orleans was the largest city in the Confederacy.

The city of Vicksburg, Mississippi, was a Confederate stronghold during the Civil War.

Union troops at Vicksburg, Mississippi, in 1863.

Farragut next took his fleet north along the Mississippi to the city of Vicksburg. From the beginning, he suffered setbacks. Farragut's ships were built to sail on the oceans. They sank too deep in the water to navigate the shallow Mississippi. Time after time, his vessels scraped against the river bottom and became stuck. He finally reached Vicksburg in late May and discovered still another problem. Confederate forts at Vicksburg were perched on bluffs some 300 feet (90 meters) above the water. Guns on Farragut's ships could not hit targets that high. Yet Confederate guns could easily shoot down on the Union fleet.

The river battle for Vicksburg stretched on into the broiling hot summer of 1862. Farragut ordered repeated attacks. The people of Vicksburg suffered bombardment, hunger, and constant fear. A Confederate officer wrote, "Loud explosions shook the city to its foundations . . . men, women, and children rushed into the streets, and amid the crash of falling houses commenced their hasty flight to the country for safety."

Unfortunately, despite the repeated attacks, Farragut was unable to take control of the city. He called off the attacks and ordered his ships to withdraw from Vicksburg.

The people of Vicksburg, Mississippi, suffered from hunger and constant fear as the battle for their city raged during the Civil War.

31

A portrait of David Farragut taken during the Civil War by a photographer from the famous studio of Mathew Brady.

Chapter Four

David Farragut's Place in History

After the Mississippi River operation, Farragut commanded fleets that blockaded southern ports. It was a duty he did not enjoy because it meant starving innocent people in the Confederate states. His most famous action in the Civil War came in August 1864, when he defied enemy guns and torpedoes and led his fleet into Mobile Bay. That operation alone established his place of glory in American history.

The Civil War ended in April 1865, after four years of terrible bloodshed. With the war over, slavery was **abolished** and the American union restored. A joyful country rewarded its heroes. In 1866, Congress named David Farragut Admiral of the Navy. The rank of full admiral was created just for him.

In 1867, Farragut commanded a United States fleet that made a peaceful visit to Europe. He dined with heads of state in Germany, France, and Russia. In England, the newspapers compared Farragut to their own naval hero, Lord Nelson. The British press called the American admiral "the Nelson of the Age."

In the summer of 1870, Farragut visited the naval yard at Portsmouth, New Hampshire. He was 69 years old, and he had been feeling weak and ill for several months. In Portsmouth, he chanced upon a warship called the *Dale,* which was launched in 1839. The old ship rested in harbor and would soon be junked. The *Dale* was a sailing ship, now **outmoded** by steam

David Farragut visited the naval yard at Portsmouth, New Hampshire, in 1870.

The Dale *(above) was a sailing ship that was outmoded by the invention of steam-powered warships.*

power. Farragut climbed aboard the *Dale* because he longed to feel a wooden deck under his feet once more. He talked to an old seaman who served as watchman and said, "This is the last time I shall ever tread the deck of a man-of-war." Farragut died at Portsmouth on August 14, 1870. The ringing of ships' bells in the harbor was probably the last sound he heard.

Some people are remembered for the deeds they did and others for words they said. Farragut's lasting fame comes from both sources. He was, perhaps, the most successful commander in the history of the United States Navy. Despite incredible odds, he led his fleet to victories at New Orleans and Mobile Bay. His words also live through the ages. Certain words have inspired generations of Americans. Facing execution, the patriot Nathan Hale said, "I only regret that I have but one life to lose for my country." When asked to surrender his ship, John Paul Jones shouted defiantly, "I have not yet begun to fight." So it was with David Farragut at Mobile Bay when he issued his order, "Damn the torpedoes. Full speed ahead!"

David Farragut served in the U.S. Navy for most of his life. In 1866, he was the first person to be awarded the rank of Admiral of the Navy.

1755: Jorge Farragut is born in Minorca on September 29.

1776: Jorge Farragut emigrates to the United States.

1801: James Glasgow Farragut is born near Nashville, Tennessee, on July 5.

1808: His mother, Elizabeth, dies, and Farragut is adopted into the David Porter family; to honor his new family, he later changes his first name to David.

1811: Ten-year-old David Glasgow Farragut goes to sea as a midshipman.

1814: Young Farragut sees naval combat for the first time as his ship, the Essex, battles a British vessel during the War of 1812.

1817: Farragut's father dies on June 4.

1823: Farragut serves under Porter's command in the Caribbean Sea.

1855: Farragut is promoted to the rank of captain in the U.S. Navy.

1861: The American Civil War begins, and Farragut sides with the northern forces.

1862: Farragut leads a fleet into the Mississippi; he forces the city of New Orleans to surrender, but is unable to conquer Vicksburg.

1864: At Mobile Bay, Alabama, Farragut issues his now famous command, "Damn the torpedoes. Full speed ahead!" and defeats his enemy.

1865: The Civil War ends.

1866: Congress names Farragut Admiral of the Navy, a rank created just for him.

1870: David Glasgow Farragut dies on August 14 in Portsmouth, New Hampshire.

abolished (uh-BOL-isht) Something that is abolished is officially done away with or ended. With the war over, slavery was abolished and the American union restored.

blockade (blok-ADE) A blockade is a closing off of traffic or supplies to and from a city. At the beginning of the war, President Abraham Lincoln announced a blockade of the entire American coast, from Virginia down to Texas.

bristled (BRISS-uhld) To be bristled means to be covered with something. The forts bristled with guns.

burly (BUR-lee) A large or muscular person is said to be burly. How could young Farragut be the boss over burly sailors who were older and far stronger than he was?

environment (en-VYE-ruhn-muhnt) All of the circumstances that influence a person's life make up his environment. The sea was an environment Farragut loved.

flotilla (flo-TI-luh) A flotilla is another word for a fleet, or group, of ships. Ironclad ships led Farragut's attacking flotilla.

loomed (LOOMD) To say that something loomed means that it was about to happen. On August 5, 1864, another bloody sea battle loomed at Mobile Bay, Alabama.

obsolete (ob-suh-LEET) Something that is outdated by a more advanced technology is obsolete. In one day, wooden battleships were made obsolete.

outmoded (out-MOHD-id) Something that is no longer useful due to advanced age is outmoded. The *Dale* was a sailing ship, now outmoded by steam power.

ram (RAM) A ram is a kind of warship that has a heavy beak at the prow, or front, that can be used to put holes in an enemy ship. The powerful, Confederate ironclad ram, the *Tennessee,* now confronted them.

Books

Anderson, Dale. *The Civil War at Sea*. Milwaukee, Wisc.: World Almanac Library, 2004.

Roop, Peter, Connie Roop, and Michael McCurdy (illustrator). *Take Command, Captain Farragut!* New York: Atheneum Books for Young Readers, 2001.

Savage, Douglas J. *Ironclads and Blockades in the Civil War*. Philadelphia: Chelsea House Publishers, 2000.

Sullivan, George. *The Civil War at Sea*. Brookfield, Conn.: Twenty-First Century Books, 2001.

Web Sites

Visit our home page for lots of links about David Farragut:

http://www.childsworld.com/links.html

Note to Parents, Teachers, and Librarians:
We routinely check our Web links to make sure they're safe, active sites—
so encourage your readers to check them out!

About the Author

R. Conrad Stein was born in Chicago. At age 18, he joined the Marine Corps and served for three years. He later attended the University of Illinois, where he graduated with a degree in history. A full-time writer, Mr. Stein has published more than 100 books for young readers. He lived in Mexico for many years, and his family still vacations in that country. The author now lives in Chicago with his wife (children's book author Deborah Kent) and their daughter, Janna.